Julian Henry Charles Fane

Tannhäuser

Or, the battle of the bards. A poem.

Julian Henry Charles Fane

Tannhäuser
Or, the battle of the bards. A poem.

ISBN/EAN: 9783337331566

Printed in Europe, USA, Canada, Australia, Japan

Cover: Foto ©Thomas Meinert / pixelio.de

More available books at **www.hansebooks.com**

TANNHÄUSER;

OR,

The Battle of the Bards.

A Poem.

BY

NEVILLE TEMPLE AND EDWARD TREVOR.

LONDON:
CHAPMAN AND HALL, 193, PICCADILLY.
1861.

THE reader is solicited to adopt the German pronunciation of TANNHÄUSER, by sounding it as if it were written, in English, "Tannho*i*ser."

TANNHÄUSER.

This is the Land, the happy valleys these,

Broad breadths of plain, blue-vein'd by many a stream,

Umbrageous hills, sweet glades, and forests fair,

O'er which our good liege, Landgrave Herman, rules.

This is Thuringia: yonder, on the heights,

Is Wartburg, seat of our dear lord's abode,

Famous through Christendom for many a feat

Of deftest knights, chief stars of chivalry,

At tourney in its courts; nor more renown'd

For deeds of Prowess than exploits of Art,

Achieved when, vocal in its Muses' hall,
The minstrel-knights their glorious jousts renew,
And for the laurel wage harmonious war.
On this side spreads the Chase in wooded slopes
And sweet acclivities; and, all beyond,
The open flats lie fruitful to the sun
Full many a league; till, dark against the sky,
Bounding the limits of our lord's domain,
The Hill of Hörsel rears his horrid front.
Woe to the man who wanders in the vast
Of those unhallow'd solitudes, if Sin,
Quickening the lust of carnal appetite,
Lurk secret in his heart: for all their caves
Echo weird strains of magic, direful-sweet,
That lap the wanton sense in blissful ease;
While through the ear a reptile music creeps,
And, blandly-busy, round about the soul
Weaves its fell web of sounds. The unhappy wight,

Thus captive made in soft and silken bands
Of tangled harmony, is led away—
Away adown the ever-darkening caves,
Away from fairness and the face of God,
Away into the mountain's mystic womb,
To where, reclining on her impious couch
All the fair length of her lascivious limbs,
Languid in light from roseate tapers flung,
Incensed with perfumes, tended on by fays,
The lustful Queen, waiting damnation, holds
Her bestial revels. The Queen of Beauty once,
A goddess call'd and worshipp'd in the days
When men their own infirmities adored,
Deeming divine who in themselves summ'd up
The full-blown passions of humanity.
Large fame and lavish service had she then,
Venus yclep'd, of all the Olympian crew
Least continent of Spirits and most fair.

So reap'd she honour of unwistful men,
Roman, or Greek, or dwellers on the plains
Of Egypt, or the isles to utmost Ind;
Till came the crack of that tremendous Doom
That sent the false gods shivering from their seats,
Shatter'd the superstitious dome that blear'd
Heaven's face to man, and on the lurid world
Let in effulgence of untainted light.
As when, laid bare beneath the delver's toil
On some huge bulk of buried masonry
In hoar Assyria, suddenly reveal'd
A chamber, gay with sculpture and the pomp
Of pictur'd tracery on its glowing walls,
No sooner breathes the wholesome heavenly air
Than fast its coloured bravery fades, and fall
Its ruin'd statues, crumbled from their crypts,
And all its gauds grow dark at sight of day;
So darken'd and to dusty ruin fell

OR, THE BATTLE OF THE BARDS.

The fleeting glories of a Pagan faith,
Bared to Truth's influences bland, and smit
Blind by the splendours of the Bethlehem Dawn.
Then from their shatter'd temple in the minds
Of men, and from their long familiar homes,
Their altars, fanes, and shrines, the sumptuous seats
Of their mendacious oracles, out-slunk
The wantons of Olympus. Forth they fled,
Forth from Dodona, Delos, and the depths
Of wooded Ida; from Athenæ forth,
Cithæron, Paphos, Thebes, and all their groves
Of oak or poplar, dismally to roam
About the new-baptizèd earth; exiled,
Bearing the curse, yet suffer'd for a space,
By Heaven's clear sapience and inscrutable ken,
To range the wide world, and assay their powers
To unregenerate redeem'd mankind :
If haply they by shadows and by shows,

Phantasmagoria, and illusions wrought
Of sight or sound by sorcery, may draw
Unwary men, or weak, into the nets
Of Satan their great Captain. She renown'd
' The fairest,' fleeing from her Cyprian isle,
Swept to the northwards many a league, and lodged
At length on Hörsel, into whose dark womb
She crept confounded. Thither soon she drew
Lewd Spirits to herself, and there abides,
Holding her devilish orgies; and has power
With siren voices crafty to compel
Into her wanton home unhappy men
Whose souls to sin are prone. The pure at heart
Natheless may roam about her pestilent hill
Untainted, proof against perfidious sounds
Within whose ears an angel ever sings
Good tidings of great joy. Nor even they,
Whose hearts are gross, and who inflamed with lust

Enter, entrapp'd by sorceries, to her cave,
Are damn'd beyond redemption. For a while,
Slaves of their bodies, in the sloughs of Sin
They roll contented, wallowing in the arms
Of their libidinous goddess. But, ere long,
Comes loathing of the sensual air they breathe,
Loathing of light unhallow'd, sickening sense
Of surfeited enjoyment; and their lips,
Spurning the reeky pasture, yearn for draughts
Of rock-rebounding rills, their eyes for sight
Of Heaven, their limbs for lengths of dewy grass :
What time sharp Conscience pricks them, and awake
Starts the requicken'd soul with all her powers,
And breaks, if so she will, the murderous spell,
Calling on God. God to her rescue sends
Voiced seraphims that lead the sinner forth
From darkness unto day, from foul embrace
Of that bloat Queen into the mother-lap

Of earth, and the caressent airs of Heaven;
Where he, by strong persistency of prayer,
By painful pilgrimage, by lengths of fast
That tame the rebel flesh, by many a night
Of vigil, days of deep repentant tears,
May cleanse his soul of her adulterate stains,
May from his sin-encrusted spirit shake
The leprous scales,—and, purely at the feet
Of his Redemption falling, may arise
Of Christ accepted. Whoso doubts the truth,
Doubting how deep divine Compassion is,
Lend to my tale a willing ear, and learn.

Full twenty summers have fled o'er the land,
A score of winters on our Landgrave's head
Have shower'd their snowy honours, since the days
When in his court no nobler knight was known,
And in his halls no happier bard was heard,

Than bright Tannhäuser. Warrior, minstrel, he
Throve for a while within the general eye,
As some king-cedar, in Crusader tales,
The stateliest growth of Lebanonian groves:
For now I sing him in his matchless prime,
Not, as in latter days, defaced and marr'd
By secret sin, and like the wasted torch
Found in the dank grass at the ghastly dawn,
After a witches' revel. He was a man
In whom prompt Nature, as in those soft climes
Where life is indolently opulent,
Blossom'd unbid to graces barely won
From tedious culture, where less kindly stars
Cold influence keep; and trothful men, who once
Look'd in his lordly, luminous eyes, and scann'd
His sinewous frame, compact of pliant power,
Aver he was the fairest-favour'd knight
That ever, in the light of ladies' looks,

Made gay these goodly halls. Oh! deeper dole,
That so august a Spirit, sphered so fair,
Should from the starry sessions of his peers
Decline, to quench so bright a brilliancy
In Hell's sick spume. Ay me, the deeper dole!

From yonder tower the wheeling lapwing loves
Beyond all others, that o'ertops the pines,
And from his one white, wistful, window stares
Into the sullen heart o' the land,—erewhile
The wandering woodman oft, at nightfall, heard
A sad, wild strain of solitary song
Float o'er the forest. Whoso heard it, paused
Compassionately, cross'd himself, and sigh'd
' Alas! poor Princess, to thy piteous moan
Heaven send sweet peace!' Heaven heard. And now
    she lies
Under the marble, 'mid the silent tombs,

Calm with her kindred; as her soul above
Rests with the saints of God.
                                The brother's child
Of our good lord the Landgrave was this maid,
And here with him abode; for in the breach
At Ascalon her sire in Holy Land
Had fallen, fighting for the Cross. These halls
Shelter'd her infancy, and here she grew
Among the shaggy barons, like the pale,
Mild-eyed, March-violet of the North, that blows
Bleak under bergs of ice. Full fair she grew,
And all men loved the rare Elizabeth;
But she, of all men, loved one man the most,
Tannhäuser, minstrel, knight, the man in whom
All mankind flower'd. Fairer growth, indeed,
Of knighthood never blossom'd to the eye;
But, furl'd beneath that florid surface, lurk'd
A vice of nature, breeding death, not life;

Such as where some rich Roman, to delight
Luxurious days with labyrinthian walks
Of rose and lily, marble fountains, forms
Wanton of Grace or Nymph, and winding frieze
With sculpture rough, hath deck'd the summer haunts
Of his voluptuous villa,—there, festoon'd
With flowers, among the Graces and the Gods,
The lurking fever glides.

      A dangerous skill,
Caught from the custom of those troubadours
That roam the wanton South, too near the homes
Of the lost gods, had crept in careless use
Among our northern bards; to play the thief
Upon the poets of a pagan time,
And steal, to purfle their embroider'd lays,
Voluptuous trappings of lascivious lore.
Hence had Tannhäuser, from of old, indulged
In song too lavish license to mislead

The sense among those fair but phantom forms
That haunt the unhallow'd past: wherefrom One Shape
Forth of the cloudy circle gradual grew
Distinct, in dissolute beauty. She of old,
Who from the idle foam uprose, to reign
In fancies all as idle,—that fair fiend,
Venus, whose temples are the veins in youth.

Now more and ever more she mix'd herself
With all his moods, and whisper'd in his walks;
Or through the misty minster, when he kneel'd
Meek on the flint, athwart the incense-smoke
She stole on sleeping sunbeams, sprinkled sounds
Of cymbals through the silver psalms, and marr'd
His adoration: most of all, whene'er
He sought to fan those fires of holy love
That, sleeping oftenest, sometimes leapt to flame,
Kindled by kindred passion in the eyes

Of sweet Elizabeth, round him rose and roll'd
That miserable magic; and, at times,
It drove him forth to wander in the waste
And desert places, there where prayerless man
Is most within the power of prowling fiends.

Time put his sickle in among the days.
Outcropp'd the coming harvest; and there came
An evening with the Princess, when they twain
Together ranged the terrace that o'erlaps
The great south garden.   All her simple hair
A single sunbeam from the sleepy west
O'erfloated; swam her soft blue eyes suffused
With tender ruth, and her meek face was moved
To one slow, serious smile, that stole to find
Its resting-place on his.

      Then, while he look'd
On that pure loveliness, within himself

He faintly felt a mystery like pure love:
For through the arid hollows of a heart
Sered by delirious dreams, the dewy sense
Of innocent worship stole. The one great word
That long had hover'd in the silent mind
Now on the lip half settled; for not yet
Had love between them been a spoken sound
For after speech to lean on; only here
And there, where scatter'd pauses strew'd their talk,
Love seem'd to o'erpoise the silence, like a star
Seen through a tender trouble of light clouds.
But, in that moment, some mysterious touch,
A thought—who knows?—a memory—something caught
Perchance from flying fancies, taking form
Among the sunset clouds, or scented gusts
Of evening through the gorgeous glooms, shrunk up
His better angel, and at once awaked
The carnal creature sleeping in the flesh.

Then died within his heart that word of life
Unspoken, which, if spoken, might have saved
The dreadful doom impending. So they twain
Parted, and nothing said: she to her tower,
There with meek wonder to renew the calm
And customary labour of the loom;
And he into the gradual-creeping dark
Which now began to draw the rooks to roost
Along the windless woods.

      His soul that eve
Shook strangely if some flickering shadow stole
Across the slopes where sunset, sleeping out
The day's last dream, yet linger'd low. Old songs
Were sweet about his brain, old fancies fair
O'erflow'd with lurid life the lonely land:
The twilight troop'd with antic shapes, and swarm'd
Above him, and the deep mysterious woods
With mystic music drew him to his doom.

So rapt, with idle and with errant foot
He wander'd on to Hörsel, and those glades
Of melancholy fame, whose poisonous glooms,
Deck'd with the gleaming hemlock, darkly fringe
The Mount of Venus.   There, a drowsy sense
Of languor seized him; and he sat him down
Among a litter of loose stones and blocks
Of broken columns, overrun with weed,
Remnants of heathen work that sometime propp'd
A pagan temple.
    Suddenly, the moon,
Slant from the shoulder of the monstrous hill,
Swung o'er a sullen lake, and softly touch'd
With light a shatter'd statue in the weed.
He lifted up his eyes, and all at once,
Bright in her baleful beauty, he beheld
The goddess of his dreams.   Beholding whom,
Lost to his love, forgetful of his faith,

And fever'd by the stimulated sense
Of reprobate desire, the madman cried:
' Descend, Dame Venus, on my soul descend!
Break up the marble sleep of those still brows
Where beauty broods! Down all my senses swim,
As yonder moon to yonder love-lit lake
Swims down in glory!'

      Hell the horrid prayer
Accorded with a curse. Scarce those wild words
Were utter'd, when like mist the marble moved,
Flusht with false life. Deep in a sleepy cloud
He seem'd to sink beneath the sumptuous face
Lean'd o'er him,—all the whiteness, all the warmth,
And all the luxury of languid limbs,
Where violet vein-streaks, lost in limpid lengths
Of snowy surface, wander faint and fine;
Whilst cymbal'd music, stol'n from underneath,
Creeps through a throbbing light that grows and glows

From glare to greater glare, until it gluts
And gulfs him in.
     And from that hour, in court,
And chase, and tilted tourney, many a month,
From mass in holy church, and mirth in hall,
From all the fair assemblage of his peers,
And all the feudatory festivals,
Men miss'd Tannhäuser.
     At the first, as when
From some great oak his goodliest branch is lopp'd,
The little noisy birds, that built about
The foliage, gather in the gap with shrill
And querulous curiosity; even so,
From all the twittering tongues that throng'd the court
Rose general hubbub of astonishment,
And vext surmise about the absent man:
Why absent? whither wander'd? on what quest
Of errant prowess?—for, as yet, none knew

His miserable fall.   But time wore on,
The wonder wore away; round absence crept
The weed of custom, and the absent one
Became at last a memory, and no more.

One heart within that memory lived aloof;
One face, remembering his, forgot to smile;
Our Landgrave's niece the old familiar ways
Walk'd like a ghost with unfamiliar looks.

Time put his sickle in among the days.
The rose burn'd out; red Autumn lit the woods;
The last snows, melting, changed to snowy clouds;
And Spring once more with incantations came
To wake the buried year.   Then did our liege,
Lord Landgrave Herman—for he loved his niece,
And lightly from her simple heart had won
The secret of lost smiles, and why she droop'd,

A wilted flower—thinking to dispel,
If that might be, her mournfulness, let cry
By heralds that, at coming Whitsuntide,
The minstrel-knights in Wartburg should convene
To hold high combat in the craft of song,
And sing before the Princess for the prize.

But, ere that time, it fell upon a day
When our good lord went forth to hunt the hart,
That he with certain of his court, 'mid whom
Was Wolfram,—once Tannhäuser's friend, himself
Among the minstrels held in high renown—
Came down the Wartburg valley, where they deem'd
To hold the hart at siege, and found him not:
But found, far down, at bottom of the glade,
Beneath a broken cross, a lonely knight
Who sat on a great stone, watching the clouds.
And Wolfram, being a little in the van

Of all his fellows, eager for the hunt,
Hurriedly ran to question of the knight
If he had view'd the hart. But when he came
To parley with him, suddenly he gave
A shout of great good cheer; for, all at once,
In that same knight he saw, and knew, though changed,
Tannhäuser, his old friend and fellow-bard.

Now, Wolfram long had loved Elizabeth
As one should love a star in heaven, who knows
The distance of it, and the reachlessness.
But when he knew Tannhäuser in her heart,
(For loving eyes in eyes beloved are swift
To search out secrets) not the less his own
Clave unto both ; and, from that time, his love
Lived like an orphan child in charity,
Whose loss came early, and is gently borne,
Too deep for tears, too constant for complaint.

And, therefore, in the absence of his friend
His inmost heart was heavy, when he saw
The shadow of that absence in the face
He loved beyond all faces upon earth.
So that when now he found that friend again
Whom he had miss'd and mourn'd, right glad was he
Both for his own and for the Princess' sake:
And ran and fell upon Tannhäuser's neck,
And all for joy constrain'd him to his heart,
Calling his fellows from the neighbouring hills,
Who, crowding, came, great hearts and open arms
To welcome back their peer. The Landgrave then,
When he perceived his well-belovèd knight,
Was passing glad, and would have question'd him
Of his long absence. But the man himself
Could answer nothing; staring with blank eyes
From face to face, then up into the blue
Bland heavens above; astonied, and like one

Who, suddenly awaking out of sleep
After sore sickness, knows his friends again,
And would peruse their faces, but breaks off
To list the frolic bleating of the lamb
In far-off fields, and wonder at the world
And all its strangeness.   Then, while the glad knights
Clung round him, wrung his hands, and dinn'd his ears
With clattering query, our fair lord himself
Unfolded how, upon the morrow morn,
There should be holden festive in his halls
High meeting of the minstrels of the land,
To sing before the Princess for the prize:
Whereto he bade him with 'O sir, be sure
There lives a young voice that shall tax your wit
To justify this absence from your friends.
We trust, at least, that you have brought us back
A score of giants' beards, or dragons' tails,
To lay them at the feet of our fair niece.

For think not, truant, that Elizabeth
Will hold you lightly quitted.'
                              At that name,
Elizabeth, he started as a man
That hears on foreign shores, from alien lips,
Some name familiar to his fatherland;
And all at once the man's heart inly yearns
For brooks that bubble, and for woods that wave
Before his father's door, while he forgets
The forms about him. So Tannhäuser mused
A little space, then falter'd: 'O my liege,
'Fares my good lady well?—I pray my lord
That I may draw me hence a little while,
For all my mind is troubled: and, indeed,
I know not if my harp have lost his skill,
But, skill'd, or skilless, it shall find some tone
To render thanks to-morrow to my lord;
To whose behests a bondsman, in so far

As my poor service holds, I will assay
To sing before the Princess for the prize.'

Then, on the morrow morn, from far and near
Flow'd in the feudatory lords. The hills
Broke out ablaze with banners, and rung loud
With tingling trumpet notes, and neighing steeds.
For all the land, elate with lusty life,
Buzz'd like a beehive in the sun; and all
The castle swarm'd from bridge to barbican
With mantle and with mail, whilst minster-bells
Rang hoarse their happy chimes, till the high noon
Clang'd from the towers. Then, o'er the platform stoled
And canopied in crimson, lightly blew
The scepter'd heralds on the silver trump
Intense sonorous music, sounding in
The knights to hall. Shrill clink'd the corridors
Through all the courts with clashing heels, or moved

With silken murmurs, and elastic sounds
Of lady laughters light; as in they flow'd
Lord, Liegeman, Peer, and Prince, and Paladin,
And dame and damsel, clad in dimpling silk
And gleaming pearl; who, while the groaning roofs
Re-echo'd royal music, swept adown
The spacious hall, with due obeisance made
To the high däis, and on glittering seats
Dropp'd one by one, like flocks of burnish'd birds
That settle down with sunset-painted plumes
On gorgeous woods. Again from the outer wall
The intermitted trumpet blared; and each
Pert page, a-tiptoe, from the benches lean'd
To see the minstrel-knights, gold-filleted,
That enter'd now the hall: Sir Mandeville,
The swan of Eisnach; Wilfrid of the Hills;
Wolfram, surnamed of Willow-brook; and next
Tannhäuser, christen'd of the Golden Harp;

With Walter of the Heron-chase; and Max,
The seer; Sir Rudolf, of the Raven-crest;
And Franz, the falconer.   They enter'd, each
In order, follow'd by a blooming boy
That bore his harp, and, pacing forward, bow'd
Before the Landgrave and Elizabeth.

Pale sat the Princess in her chair of state,
Perusing with fix'd eyes, that all belied
Her throbbing heart, the carven architrave,
Whereon the intricate much-vex'd design
Of leaf and stem disintertwined itself
With infinite laboriousness, at last
Escaping in a flight of angel forms;
As tho' the carver's thought had been to show
The weary struggle of the soul to free
Her flight from earth's bewilderment, and all
That frets her in the flesh.   But when, erewhile,

The minstrels enter'd, and Tannhäuser bow'd
Before the däis, the Landgrave, at her side,
Saw, as he mused what theme to give for song,
The pallid forehead of Elizabeth
Flush to the fair roots of her golden hair,
And thought within himself: 'Our knight delays
To own a love that aims so near our throne;
Hence, haply, this late absence from our court,
And those bewilder'd moods which I have mark'd:
But since love lightly catches, where it can,
At any means to make itself approved,
And since the singer may to song confide
What the man dares not trust to simple speech,
I, therefore, so to ease two hearts at once,
And signify our favour unto both,
Will to our well-belovèd minstrels give
No theme less sweet than Love: for, surely, he
That loves the best, will sing the best, and bear

The prize from all.'   Therewith the Landgrave rose,
And all the murmuring Hall was hush'd to hear.

' O well-belovèd minstrels, in my mind
I do embrace you all, and heartily
Bid you a lavish welcome to these halls.
Oft have you flooded this fair space with song,
Waked these voiced walls, and vocal made yon roof,
As waves of surging music lapp'd against
Its resonant rafters.   Often have your strains
Ennobled souls of true nobility,
Rapt by your perfect pleadings in the cause
Of all things pure unto a purer sense
Of their exceeding loveliness.   No power
Is subtler o'er the spirit of man than Song—
Sweet echo of great thoughts, that, in the mind
Of him who hears congenial echoes waking,
Remultiplies the praise of what is good.

Song cheers the emulous spirit to the top

Of Virtue's rugged steep, from whence, all heights

Of human worth attain'd, the mortal may

Conjecture of God's unattainable,

Which is Perfection.—Faith, with her sisters twain

Of Hope and Charity, ye oft have sung,

And loyal Truth have lauded, and have wreathed

A coronal of music round the brows

Of stainless Chastity; nor less have praised

High-minded Valour, in whose righteous hand

Burns the great sword of flaming Fortitude,

And have stirr'd up to deeds of high emprize

Our noble knights (yourselves among the noblest)

Whether on German soil for me, their prince,

Fighting, or in the Land of Christ for God.

Sing ye to-day another theme; to-day

Within our glad society we see,

To fellowship of loving friends restored,

A long-miss'd face; and hungerly our ears
Wait the melodious murmurs of a harp
That wont to feed them daintily. What drew
Our singer forth, and led the fairest light
Of all our galaxy to swerve astray
From his fix'd orbit, and what now respheres,
After deflection long, our errant orb,
Implies a secret that the subtle power
Of Song, perchance, may solve. Be then your theme
As universal as the heart of man,
Giving you scope to touch its deepest depths,
Its highest heights, and reverently to explore
Its mystery of mysteries. Sing of Love:
Tell us, ye noble poets, from what source
Springs the prime passion; to what goal it tends;
Sing it how brave, how beautiful, how bright,
In essence how ethereal, in effect
How palpable, how human yet divine.

Up! up! loved singers, smite into the chords,
The lists are open'd, set your lays in rest,
And who of Love best chants the perfect praise,
Him shall Elizabeth as conqueror hail
And round his royal temples bind the bays.'

He said, and sat.   And from the middle-hall
Four pages, bearers of the blazon'd urn
That held the name-scrolls of the listed bards,
Moved to Elizabeth.   Daintily her hand
Dipp'd in the bowl, and one drawn scroll deliver'd
Back to the pages, who, perusing, cried:
' Sir Wolfram of the Willow-brook,—begin.'

Up-rose the gentle singer—he whose lays,
Melodious-melancholy, through the Land
Live to this day—and, fair obeisance made,
Assumed his harp and stood in act to sing.

Awhile, his dreamy fingers o'er the chords
Wander'd at will, and to the roof was turn'd
His meditative face; till, suddenly,
A soft light from his spiritual eyes
Broke, and his canticle he thus began :

'Love among the saints of God,
  Love within the hearts of men,
Love in every kindly sod
  That breeds a violet in the glen;
Love in heaven, and Love on earth,
  Love in all the amorous air;
Whence comes Love? ah! tell me where
  Had such a gracious Presence birth?
Lift thy thoughts to Him, all-knowing,
  In the hallow'd courts above;
From His throne, for ever flowing,
  Springs the fountain of all Love :

Down to earth the stream descending
Meets the hills, and murmurs then,
In a myriad channels wending,
Through the happy haunts of men.
Blessèd ye, earth's sons and daughters,
Love among you flowing free;
Guard, oh! guard its sacred waters,
Tend on them religiously:
Let them through your hearts steal sweetly,
With the Spirit, wise and bland,
Minister unto them meetly,
Touch them not with carnal hand.

' Maiden, fashion'd so divinely,
Whom I worship from afar,
Smile thou on my soul benignly,
Sweet, my solitary star:
Gentle harbinger of gladness,

Still be with me on the way;
Only soother of my sadness,
Always near, though far away :
Always near, since first upon me
Fell thy brightness from above,
And my troubled heart within me
Felt the sudden flow of Love;
At thy sight that gushing river
Paused, and fell to perfect rest,
And the pool of Love for ever
Took thy image to its breast.

' Let me keep my passion purely,
Guard its waters free from blame,
Hallow Love, as knowing surely
It returneth whence it came ;
From all channels, good or evil,
Love, to its pure source enticed,

OR, THE BATTLE OF THE BARDS.

Finds its own immortal level
In the charity of Christ.

Ye who hear, behold the river,
Whence it cometh, whither goes;
Glory be to God, the Giver,
From whose grace the fountain flows;
Flows and spreads through all creation,
Counter-charm of every curse,
Love, the waters of Salvation,
Flowing through the universe!'

And still the rapt bard, though his voice had ceased,
And all the Hall had murmur'd into praise,
Pursued his plaintive theme among the chords,
Blending with instinct fine the intricate throng
Of thoughts that flow'd beneath his touch to find
Harmonious resolution.   As he closed,

Tannhäuser rising, fretted with delay,
Sent flying fingers o'er the strings, and sang:

  ' Love be my theme! Sing her awake,
    My harp, for she hath tamely slept
    In Wolfram's song, a stagnant lake
    O'er which a shivering star hath crept.

  ' Awake, dull waters, from your sleep,
    Rise, Love, from thy delicious well,
    A fountain!—yea, but flowing deep
    With nectar and with hydromel;

  ' With gurgling murmurs sweet, that teach
    My soul a sleep-distracting dream,
    Till on the marge I lie, and reach
    My longing lips towards the stream;

  ' Whose waves leap upwards to the brink,
    With drowning kisses to invite
    And drag me, willing, down to drink
    Delirious draughts of rare Delight;

' Who careless drink, as knowing well
　The happy pastime shall not tire,
　For Love is inexhaustible,
　And all-unfailing my Desire.

' Love's fountain-marge is fairly spread
　With every incense-flower that blows,
　With flossy sedge, and moss that grows
　For fervid limbs a dewy bed;

' And fays and fairies flit and wend
　To keep the sweet stream flowing free,
　And on Love's languid votary
　The little elves delighted tend;

' And bring him honey-dews to sip,
　Rare balms to cool him after play,
　Or with sweet unguents smooth away
　The kiss-crease on his ruffled lip;

' And lilywhite his limbs they lave,
　　And roses in his cheeks renew,
　　That he, refresh'd, return to glue
　　His lips to Love's caressent wave;

' And feel, in that immortal kiss,
　　His mortal instincts die the death,
　　And human fancy fade beneath
　　The taste of unimagined bliss!

' Thus, gentle audience, since your ear
　　Best loves a metaphoric lay,
　　Of mighty Love I warble here
　　In figures, such as Fancy may:

' Now know ye how of Love I think
　　As of a fountain, failing never,
　　On whose soft marge I lie, and drink
　　Delicious draughts of Joy for ever.'

Abrupt he ceased, and sat. And for a space,
No longer than the subtle lightning rests

Upon a sultry cloud at eventide,

The Princess smiled, and on her parted lips

Hung inarticulate applause; but she

Sudden was ware that all the hall was mute

With blank disapprobation; and her smile

Died, and vague fear was quicken'd in her heart

As Walter of the Heron-chase began:

 'O fountain ever fair and bright,
  He hath beheld thee, source of Love,
  Who sung thee springing from above,
  Celestial from the founts of Light;

 'But he who from thy waters rare
  Hath thought to drain a gross delight,
  Blind in his spiritual sight,
  Hath ne'er beheld thee, fountain fair!

 'Hath never seen the silver glow
  Of thy glad waves, crystalline clear,
  Hath never heard within his ear
  The music of thy murmurous flow.

'The essence of all Good thou art,
   Thy waters are immortal Ruth,
   Thy murmurs are the voice of Truth,
   And music in the human heart:

'Thou yieldest Faith that soars on high,
   And Sympathy that dwells on earth;
   The tender trust in human worth,
   The hope that lives beyond the sky.

'Oh! waters of the living Word,
   Oh! fair vouchsafed us from above,
   Oh! fountain of immortal Love
   What song of thee erewhile I heard!

'Learn, sacrilegious bard, from me
   How all ignoble was thy strain,
   That sought with trivial song to stain
   The fountain of Love's purity;

'That fountain thou hast never found,
   And should'st thou come with lips of fire
   To slake the thirst of brute Desire,
   'Twould shrink and shrivel to the ground:

' Who seeks in Love's pure stream to lave
    His gross heart finds damnation near;
    Who laves in Love his spirit clear
    Shall win Salvation from the wave.'

And now again, as when the plaintive lay

Of Wolfram warbled to harmonious close,

The crowd grew glad with plaudits; and again

Tannhäuser, ruffled, rose his height, and smote

Rude in the chords his prelude of reply :

' What Love is this that melts with Ruth,
    Whose murmurs are the voice of Truth?
    Ye dazèd singers, cease to dream,
    And learn of me your human theme :
    Of that great Passion at whose feet
    The vassal-world lies low,
    Of Love the mighty, Love the sweet,
    I sing, who reigns below;

Who makes men fierce, tame, wild, or kind,
  Sovran of every mood,
Who rules the heart, and rules the mind,
  And courses through the blood:
Slave, of that lavish Power I sing,
  Dispenser of all good,
Whose pleasure-fountain is the spring
  Of sole beatitude.

' Sing ye of Love ye ne'er possess'd
  In wretched tropes—a vain employment!
I sing the passion in my breast,
  And know Love only in Enjoyment.'

To whom, while all the rustling hall was moved
With stormy indignation, stern up-rose,
Sharp in retort, Sir Wilfrid of the hills:

  ' Up, minstrels! rally to the cry
    Of outraged Love and Loyalty;

Drive on this slanderer, all the throng,
And slay him in a storm of song.
Oh lecher! shall I sing to thee
Of Love's untainted purity,
Of simple Faith, and tender Ruth,
Of Chastity and loyal Truth?
As well sing Day's resplendent birth
To the blind mole that delves the earth
As seek from gross hearts, slough'd in sin,
Approval of pure Love to win!
Rather from thee I'll wring applause
For Love, the Avenger of his cause;
Great Love, the chivalrous and strong,
To whose wide grasp all arms belong,
The lance, the battle-axe, and thong,—
And eke the mastery in song.

'Love in my heart in all the pride
Of kinghood sits, and at his side,

To do the bidding of his lord,
Martial Valour holds the sword;
He strikes for Honour, in the name
Of Virtue and fair woman's fame,
And bids me shed my dearest blood
To venge aspersèd maidenhood:
Who soils her with licentious lie,
Him will I hew both hip and thigh,
Or in her cause will dearly die.
But thou, who in thy flashy song
Hast sought to do *all* Honour wrong,
Pass on,—I will not stoop my crest
To smite thee, nor lay lance in rest.
Thy brawling words, of riot born,
Are worthy only of my scorn;
Thus at thy ears this song I fling,
Which in thy heart may plant its sting,
If ruin'd Conscience yet may wring
Remorse from such a guilty thing.'

Scarce from his lips had parted the last word

When, through the rapturous praise that rang around,

Fierce from his seat up-rising, red with rage,

With scornful lip, and contumelious eye,

Tannhäuser clang'd among the chords, and sang:

' Floutest thou me, thou grisly Bard?
   Beware, lest I the just reward
   On thy puff'd insolence bestow,
   And cleave thee with my falchion's blow,—
   When I in song have laid thee low.
   I serve a Mistress mightier far
   Than tinkling rill, or twinkling star,
   And, as in my great Passion's glow
   Thy passion-dream will melt like snow,
   So I, Love's champion, at her call,

Will make thee shrink in field or hall,
And roll before me like a ball.

' Thou pauper-minded pedant dim,
Thou starveling-soul, lean heart and grim,
Wouldst thou of Love the praises hymn?
Then let the gaunt hyena howl
In praise of Pity; let the owl
Whoop the high glories of the noon,
And the hoarse chough becroak the moon!
What canst thou prate of Love? I trow
She never graced thy open brow,
Nor flush'd thy cheek, nor blossom'd fair
Upon thy parted lips; nor e'er
Bade unpent passion wildly start
Through the forced portals of thy heart
To stream in triumph from thine eye,
Or else delicious death to die
On other lips, in sigh on sigh.

'Of Love, dispenser of all bliss,
Of Love, that crowns me with a kiss,
I here proclaim me champion-knight;
And in her cause will dearly fight
With sword or song, in hall or plain,
And make the welkin ring again
With my fierce blows, or fervent strain.
But for such Love, as thou canst feel,
Thou wisely hast abjured the steel,
Averse to lay thy hand on hilt,
Or in her honour ride a tilt:
Tame Love full tamely may'st thou jilt,
And keep bone whole, and blood unspilt.'

Outflash'd Sir Wilfrid's weapon, and outleapt
From every angry eye a thousand darts
Of unsheath'd indignation, and a shout
Went up among the rafters, and the Hall
Sway'd to and fro with tumult; till the voice

Of our liege lord roared 'Peace!' and, 'midst the clang
Of those who parted the incensèd bards,
Sounded the harp of Wolfram. Calm he stood,
He only calm of all the brawling crowd,
Which yet, as is its wont, contagion caught
From neighbouring nobleness, and a stillness fell
On all, and in the stillness soft he sang:

 'Oh! from your sacred seats look down,
  Angels and ministers of good;
  With sanctity our spirits crown,
  And crush the vices of the blood!

 'Open our hearts and set them free,
  That heavenly light may enter in;
  And from this fair society
  Obliterate the taint of sin.

 'Thee, holy Love, I bid arise
  Propitious to my votive lay;
  Shine thou upon our darken'd eyes,
  And lead us on the perfect way;

'As, in the likeness of a Star,
  Thou once arosest, guidance meet,
  And led'st the sages from afar
  To sit at holy Jesu's feet:

'So guide us, safe from Satan's snares,
  Shine out, sweet Star, around, above,
  Till we have scaled the mighty stairs,
  And reach'd thy mansions, Heavenly Love!'

Then, while great shouts went up of 'Give the prize
To Wolfram,' leapt Tannhäuser from his seat,
Fierce passion flaming from his lustrous orbs.
And, as a sinner, desperate to add
Depth to damnation by one latest crime,
Dies boastful of his blasphemies—even so,
Tannhäuser, conscious of the last disgrace
Incurr'd by such song in such company,
Intent to vaunt the vastness of his sin,
Thus, as in ecstacy, the song renew'd:

'Goddess of Beauty, thee I hymn,
 And ever worship at thy shrine;
 Thou, who on mortal senses dim
 Descending, makest man divine.

'Who hath embraced thee on thy throne,
 And pastured on thy royal kiss,
 He, happy, knows, and knows alone,
 Love's full beatitude of bliss.

'Grim bards, of Love who nothing know,
 Now cease the unequal strife between us;
 Dare as I dared ; to Hörsel go,
 And taste Love on the lips of Venus.'

Up-rose on every side and rustled down
The affrighted dames; and, like the shuddering crowd
Of particolour'd leaves that flits before
The gust of mid October, all at once
A hundred jewell'd shoulders, huddling, swept

The hall, and slanted to the doors, and fled
Before the storm, which now from shaggy brows
'Gan dart indignant lightnings. One alone
Of all that awe-struck womanhood remain'd,
The Princess. She, a purple hairbell frail,
That, swathed with whirlwind, to the bleak rock clings
When half a forest falls before the blast,
Rooted in utter wretchedness, and robed
In mockery of splendid state, still sat ;
Still watch'd the waste that widen'd in her life ;
And look'd as one that in a nightmare hangs
Upon an edge of horror, while from beneath
The creeping billow of calamity
Sprays all his hair with cold ; but hand or foot
He may not move, because the formless Fear
Gapes vast behind him. Grief within the void
Of her stark eyes stood tearless : terror blanch'd

Her countenance; and, over cloudy brows,
The shaken diamond made a restless light,
And trembled as the trembling star that hangs
O'er Cassiopeïa i' the windy north.

But now, from farthest end to end of all
The sullen movement swarming underneath,
Uproll'd deep hollow groans of growing wrath.
And, where erewhile in rainbow crescent ranged
The bright-eyed beauties of the court, fast throng'd
Faces inflamed with wrath, that rose and fell
Tumultuously gathering from between
Sharp-slanting lanes of steel. For every sword
Flash'd bare upon a sudden; and over these,
Through the wide bursten doors the sinking sun
Stream'd lurid, lighting up that steely sea;
Which, spotted white with foamy plumes, and ridged
With glittering iron, clash'd together and closed

About Tannhäuser. Careless of the wrath
Roused by his own rash song, the singer stood;
Rapt in remembrance, or by fancy fool'd
A visionary Venus to pursue,
With eyes that roam'd in rapture the blank air.
Until the sharp light of a hundred swords
Smote on the fatal trance, and scatter'd all
Its fervid fascination. Swift from sheath
Then leapt the glaive and glitter'd in his hand
And warily, with eye upon the watch,
Receding to the mighty main support
That, from the centre, propp'd the ponderous roof,
These, based against the pillar, fronting full
His sudden foes, he rested resolute,
Waiting assault.
        But, hollow as a bell,
That tolls for tempest from a storm-clad tower,
Rang through the jangling shock of arms and men

The loud voice of the Landgrave. Wide he swept
The solemn sceptre, crying 'Peace!' then said:

'Ye Lieges of Thuringia! whose just scorn,
In judgment sitting on your righteous brows,
Would seem to have forecast the dubious doom
Awaiting our decision; ye have heard,
Not wrung by torture from reluctant lips,
Nor yet breathed forth with penitential pain
In prayer for pardon, nay, but rather fledged
And barb'd with boastful insolence, such a crime
Confest, as turns to burning coals of wrath
The dewy eyes of Pity, nor to Hope
One refuge spares, save such as rests perchance
Within the bounteous bosom of the Church;
Who, caring for the frailty of her flock,
Holds mercy measureless as heaven is high.
Shuddering, ourselves have listen'd to what breaks

All bonds that bound to this unhappy man
The covenanted courtesies of knights,
The loyalties of lives by faith knit fast
In spiritual communion. What behoves,
After deliberation, to award
In sentence, I to your high council leave,
Undoubting. What may mitigate in aught
The weight of this acknowledged infamy
Weigh with due balance. What to justice stern
Mild-minded mercy yet may reconcile
Search inly. Not with rashness, not in wrath,
Invoking from the right hand of high God
His dread irrevocable angel, Death;
Yet not unwary how one spark of hell,
If unextinguish'd, down the night of time
May, like the wreckers' beacon from the reefs,
Lure many to destruction: nor indeed
Unmindful of the doom by fire or steel
This realm's supreme tribunals have reserved

For those that, dealing in damnation, hold
Dark commerce with the common foe of man.
Weigh you in all its circumstance this crime:
And, worthily judging, though your judgment be
As sharp as conscience, be it as conscience clear.'

He ended: and a bitter interval
Of silence o'er the solemn hall congeal'd,
Like frost on a waste water, in a place
Where rocks confront each other. Marshall'd round,
Black-bearded cheek and chin, with hand on heft,
Bent o'er the pommels of their planted swords,
A dreary cirque of faces ominous,
The sullen barons on each other stared
Significant. As, ere the storm descends
Upon a Druid grove, the great trees stand
Looking one way, and stiller than their wont,
Until the thunder, rolling, frees the wind

That rocks them altogether; even so,
That savage circle of grim-gnarlèd men,
Awhile in silence storing stormy thoughts,
Stood breathless; till a murmur moved them all,
And louder growing, and louder, burst at last
To a universal irrepressible roar
Of voices roaring, 'Let him die the death!'
And, in that roar released, a hundred swords
Rush'd forward, and in narrowing circle sloped
Sharp rims of shining horror round the doom'd,
Undaunted minstrel. Then a piteous cry;
And from the purple baldachin down sprang
The Princess, gleaming like a ghost, and slid
Among the swords, and standing in the midst
Swept a wild arm of prohibition forth.
Cowering, recoil'd the angry, baffled surge,
Leaving on either side a horrid hedge
Of rifted glare, as when the Red Sea waves

Hung heap'd and sunder'd, ere they roaring fell
On Egypt's chariots. So there came a hush;
And in the hush her voice, heavy with scorn:

' Or shall I call you men? or beasts? who seem
No nobler than the bloodhound and the wolf
Which scorn to prey upon their proper kind!
Christians I will not call you! who defraud
That much-misapprehended holy name
Of reverence due by such a deed as, done,
Will clash against the charities of Christ,
And make a marr'd thing and a mockery
Of the fair face of Mercy. You dull hearts,
And hard! have ye no pity for yourselves?
For man no pity? man whose common cause
Is shamed and sadden'd by the stain that falls
Upon a noble nature! You blind hands,
Thrust out so fast to smite a fallen friend!

Did ye not all conspire, whilst yet he stood
The stateliest soul among you, to set forth
And fix him in the foremost ranks of men?
Content that he, your best, should bear the brunt,
And head the van against the scornful fiend
That will not waste his weapons on the herd,
But saves them for the noblest. And shall Hell
Triumph through you, that triumph in the shame
Of this eclipse that blots your brightest out,
And leaves you dark in his extinguish'd light?
Oh, who that lives but hath within his heart
Some cause to dread the suddenness of death?
And God is merciful; and suffers us,
Even for our sins' sake; and doth spare us time,
Time to grow ready, time to take farewell!
And sends us monitors and ministers—
Old age, that steals the fullness from the veins;
And griefs, that take the glory from the eyes;
And pains, that bring us timely news of death;
And tears, that teach us to be glad of him.

For who can take farewell of all his sins

On such a sudden summons to the grave?

Against high Heaven hath this man sinn'd, or you?

Oh, if it be against high Heaven, to Heaven

Remit the compt! lest, from the armoury

Of The Eternal Justice ye pluck down,

Heedless, that bolt The Highest yet withholds

From this low-fallen head,—how fall'n! how low!

Yet not so fall'n, not so low fall'n, but what

Divine Redemption, reaching everywhere,

May reach at last even to this wretchedness,

And, out of late repentance, raise it up

With pardon into peace.'

                                    She paused: she touch'd,

As with an angel's finger, him whose pride

Obdurate now had yielded, and he lay,

Vanquish'd by Pity, broken at her feet.

She, lingering, waited answer, but none came

Across the silence. And again she spake:

' Oh, not for him alone, and not for that
Which to remember now makes life for me
A wilderness of homeless griefs, I plead
Before you; but, O Princes, for yourselves;
For all that in your nobler nature stirs
To vindicate Forgiveness and enlarge
The lovely laws of Pity! Which of you,
Here in the witness of all-judging God,
Stands spotless? Which of you will boast himself
More miserably injured by this man
Than I, whose heart of all that lived in it
He hath untenanted? Oh horrible!
Unheard of! from the blessèd lap of life
To send the soul, asleep in all her sins,
Down to perdition! Be not yours the hands
To do this desperate wrong in sight of all
The ruthful faces of the Saints in Heaven.'

She passionately pleading thus, her voice
Over their hearts moved like that earnest wind
That, labouring long against some great night-cloud,
Sets free, at last, a solitary star,
Then sinks; but leaves the night not all forlorn
Ere the soft rain o'ercomes it.
                              This long while
Wolfram, whose harp and voice were overborne
By burly brawlers in the turbulence
That shook that stormy senate, stood apart
With vainly-vigilant eye, and writhen hands,
All in mute trouble: too gentle to approve,
Too gentle to prevent, what pass'd: and still
Divided in himself 'twixt sharpest grief
To see his friend so fallen, and a drear
Strange horror of the crime whereby he fell.
So, like a headland light that down dark waves
Shines o'er some sinking ship it fails to save,

Look'd the pale singer down the lurid hall.

But when the pure voice of Elizabeth

Ceased, and clearlighted all with noble thoughts

Her face glow'd as an angel's, the sweet Bard,

Whose generous heart had scaled with that loved voice

Up to the lofty levels where it ceased,

Stood forth, and from the dubious silence caught

And carried up the purpose of her prayer;

And drew it out, and drove it to the heart,

And clench'd it with conviction in the mind,

And fix'd it firm in judgment.

      From deep muse

The Landgrave started, toward Tannhäuser strode,

And, standing o'er him with an eye wherein

Salt sorrow and a moody pity gleam'd,

Spake hoarse of utterance:

      'Arise! go forth!

Go from us, mantled in the shames which make

Thee, stranger whom mine eye henceforth abhors,
The mockery of the man I loved, and mourn.
Go from these halls yet holy with the voice
Of her whose intercession for thy sake,—
If any sacred sorrow yet survive
All ruin'd virtues,—in remorse shall steep
The memory of her wrongs. For thee remains
One hope, unhappiest! reject it not.
There goeth a holy pilgrimage to Rome,
Which not yet from the borders of our land
Is parted; pious souls and meek, whom thou
Haply may'st join, and of those holy hands,
Which sole have power to bind or loose, receive
Remission of thy sin. For save alone
The hand of Christ's high Vicar upon earth
A hurt so heinous what may heal? What save
A soul so fall'n? Go forth upon thy ways,
Which are not ours: for we no more may mix

Congenial minds in converse sweet, no more
Together pace these halls, nor ever hear
Thy harp as once when all was pure and glad,
Among the days which have been. All thy paths
Henceforth be paths of penitence and prayer,
Whilst over ours thy memory moving makes
A shadow, and a silence in our talk.
Get thee from hence, O all that now remains
Of one we honour'd! Till the hand that holds
The keys of heaven hath ope'd for thee the doors
Of life in that far distance, let mine eye
See thee no more. Go from us!'

                        Even then,
Even whilst he spake, like some sweet miracle,
From darkening lands that glimmer'd through the doors
Came, faintly heard along the filmy air
That bore it floating near, a choral chant

Of pilgrims pacing by the castle wall;
And '*salvum me fac Domine*' they sung
Sonorous, in the ghostly going out
Of the red-litten eve along the land.

Then, like a hand across the heart of him
That heard it moved that music from afar,
And beckon'd forth the better hope which leads
A man's life up along the rugged road
Of high resolve. Tannhäuser moved, as moves
The folded serpent smitten by the spring
And stirr'd with sudden sunlight, when he casts
His spotted skin, and, renovated, gleams
With novel hues. One lingering long look,
Wild with remorse and vague with vast regrets,
He lifted to Elizabeth. His thoughts
Were then as those dumb creatures in their pain
That make a language of a look. He toss'd

Aloft his arms, and down to the great doors
With droop'd brows striding, groan'd 'To Rome! to Rome!'
Whilst the deep hall behind him caught the cry
And drove it clamorous after him, from all
Its hollow roofs reverberating 'Rome!'

A fleeting darkness thro' the lurid arch;
A flying form along the glare beyond;
And he was gone. The scowling Eve reach'd out
Across the hills a fiery arm, and took
Tannhäuser to her, like a sudden death.

So ended that great Battle of the Bards,
Whereof some rumour to the end of time
Will echo in this land.
                      And, voided now
Of all his multitudes, the mighty Hall
Dumb, dismally dispageanted, laid bare

His ghostly galleries to the mournful moon;
And Night came down, and Silence, and the twain
Mingled beneath the starlight. Wheel'd at will
The flitter-wingèd bat round lonely towers
Where, one by one, from darkening casements died
The taper's shine; the howlet from the hills
Whoop'd: and Elizabeth, alone with Night
And Silence, and the Ghost of her slain youth,
Lay lost among the ruins of that day.

As when the buffeting gusts, that adverse blow
Over the Caribbean Sea, conspire
Conflicting breaths, and, savagely begot,
The fierce tornado rotatory wheels,
Or sweeps centripetal, or, all forces join'd,
Whirls circling o'er the madden'd waves, and they
Lift up their foaming backs beneath the keel
Of some frail vessel, and, careering high

Over a sunken rock, with a sudden plunge
Confound her,—stunn'd and strain'd, upon the peak
Poising one moment, ere she forward fall
To float, dishelm'd, a wreck upon the waves:
So rose, engender'd by what furious blasts
Of passion, that fell hurricane that swept
Elizabeth to her doom, and left her now
A helmless hull upon the savage seas
Of life, without an aim, to float forlorn.

Longwhile, still shuddering from the shock that jarr'd
The bases of her being, piteous wreck
Of ruin'd hopes, upon her couch she lay,
Of life and time oblivious; all her mind,
Lock'd in a rigid agony of grief,
Clasping, convulsed, its unwept woe; her heart
Writhing and riven; and her burthen'd brain
Blind with the weight of tears that would not flow.

But when, at last, the healing hand of Time
Had wrought repair upon her shatter'd frame;
And those unskill'd physicians of the mind—
Importunate, fond friends, a host of kin—
Drew her perforce from solitude, she pass'd
Back to the world, and walk'd its weary ways
With dull mechanic motions, such as make
A mockery of life. Yet gave she never,
By weeping or by wailing, outward sign
Of that great inward agony that she bore;
For she was not of those whose sternest sorrow
Outpours in plaints, or weeps itself in dew;
Not passionate she, nor of the happy souls
Whose grief comes temper'd with the gift of tears.

So, through long weeks and many a weary moon,
Silent and self-involved, without a sigh,
She suffer'd. There, whence consolation comes,

She sought it—at the foot of Jesu's cross,
And on the bosom of the Virgin-spouse,
And in communion with the blessèd Saints.
But chief for him she pray'd whose grievous sin
Had wrought her desolation; God besought
To touch the leprous soul and make it clean;
And sued the Heavenly Pastor to recall
The lost sheep, wander'd from the pleasant ways,
Back to the pasture of the paths of peace.
So thrice a day, what time the blushing morn
Crimson'd the orient sky, and when the sun
Glared from mid-heaven or welter'd in the west,
Fervent she pray'd; nor in the night forewent
Her vigils; till at last from prayer she drew
A calm into her soul, and in that calm
Heard a low whisper—like the breeze that breaks
The deep peace of the forest ere the chirp
Of earliest bird salutes the advent Day—
Thrill through her, herald of the dawn of Hope.

Then most she loved from forth her leafy tower
Listless to watch the irrevocable clouds
Roll on, and daylight waste itself away
Along those dreaming woods, whence evermore
She mused, ' He will return ;' and fondly wove
Her webs of wistful fantasy till the moon
Was high in heaven, and in its light she kneel'd,
A faded watcher through the weary night,
A meek, sweet statue at the silver shrines,
In deep, perpetual prayer for him she loved.

And from the pitying Sisterhood of Saints
Haply that prayer shall win an angel down
To be his unseen minister, and draw
A drowning conscience from the deeps of Hell.

Time put his sickle in among the days.
Blithe Summer came, and into dimples danced

The fair and fructifying Earth, anon
Showering the gather'd guerdon of her play
Into the lap of Autumn; Autumn stored
The gift, piled ready to the palsied hand
Of blind and begging Winter; and when he
Closed his well-provender'd days, Spring lightly came
And scatter'd sweets upon his sullen grave.
And twice the seasons pass'd, the sisters three
Doing glad service for their hoary brother,
And twice twelve moons had wax'd and waned, and twice
The weary world had pilgrim'd round the sun,
When from the outskirts of the land there came
Rumour of footsore penitents from Rome
Returning, jubilant of remitted sin.

So chanced it, on a silent April eve
The westering sun along the Wartburg vale

Shot level beams, and into glory touch'd
The image of Madonna—where it stands
Hard by the common way that climbs the steep—
The image of Madonna, and the face
Of meek Elizabeth turn'd towards the Queen
Of Sorrows, sorrowful in patient prayer;
When, through the silence and the sleepy leaves,
A breeze blew up the vale, and on the breeze
Floated a plaintive music. She that heard,
Trembled; the prayer upon her parted lips
Suspended hung, and one swift hand she press'd
Against the palpitating heart whose throbs
Confused the cunning of her ears. Ah God!
Was this the voice of her returning joy?
The psalm of shriven pilgrims to their homes
Returning? Ay! it swells upon the breeze
The '*Nunc Dimittis*' of glad souls that sue
After salvation seen to part in peace.

Then up she sprung, and to a neighbouring copse
Swift as a startled hind, when the ghostly moon
Draws sudden o'er the silver'd heather-bells
The monstrous shadow of a cloud, she sped;
Pausing, low-crouch'd, within a maze of shrubs,
Whose emerald slivers fringed the rugged way
So broad, the pilgrim's garments as they passed
Would brush the leaves that hid her. And anon
They came in double rank, and two by two,
With cumber'd steps, with haggard gait that told
Of bodily toil and trouble, with besoil'd
And tatter'd garments; natheless with glad eyes,
Whence look'd the soul disburthen'd of her sin,
Climbing the rude path, two by two they came.
And she, that watch'd with what intensest gaze
Them coming, saw old faces that she knew,
And every face turn'd skywards, while the lips
Pour'd out the heavenly psalm, and every soul

Sitting seraphic in the upturn'd eyes
With holy fervour rapt upon the song.
And still they came and pass'd, and still she gazed;
And still she thought, 'Now comes he!' and the chant
Went heavenwards, and the filèd pilgrims fared
Beside her, till their tale well-nigh was told.
Then o'er her soul a shuddering horror crept,
And, in that agony of mind that makes
Doubt more intolerable than despair,
With sudden hand she brush'd aside the sprays,
And from the thicket lean'd and look'd. The last
Of all the pilgrims stood within the ken
Of her keen gaze—save him all scann'd, and he
No sooner scann'd than cancell'd from her eyes
By vivid lids swept down to lash away
Him hateful, being other than she sought.
So for a space, blind with dismay, she paused
But, he approaching, from the thicket leapt,

Clutch'd with wrung hands his robe, and gasp'd, 'The
    knight
'That with you went, returns not?' In his psalm
The fervid pilgrim made no pause, yet gazed
At his wild questioner, intelligent
Of her demand, and shook his head and pass'd.
Then she, with that mute answer stabb'd to the heart,
Sprung forward, clutch'd him yet once more, and cried,
'In Mary's name, and in the name of God,
Received the knight his shrift?' And, once again,
The pilgrim, sorrowful, shook his head and sigh'd,
Sigh'd in the singing of his psalm, and pass'd.

Then prone she fell upon her face, and prone
Within her mind Hope's shatter'd fabric fell—
The dear and delicate fabric of frail Hope
Wrought by the simple cunning of her thoughts,
That, labouring long, through many a dreamy day

And many a vigil of the wakeful night,

Piecemeal had rear'd it, patiently, with pain,

From out the ruins of her ancient peace.

O, ancient Peace! that never shalt return;

O, ruin'd Hope! O, Fancy! over-fond,

Futile artificer that build'st on air,

Marr'd is thy handiwork, and thou shalt please

With plastic fantasies her soul no more.

So lay she cold against the callous ground,

Her pale face pillow'd on a stone, her eyes

Wide open, fix'd into a ghastly stare

That knew no speculation; for her mind

Was dark, and all her faculty of thought

Compassionately cancell'd. But she lay

Not in the embrace of loyal Death, who keeps

His bride for ever, but in treacherous arms

Of Sleep that, sated, will restore to Grief

Her, snatch'd a sweet space from his cruel clutch.
So lay she cold against the callous ground,
And none was near to heed her, as the sun,
About him drawing the vast-skirted clouds,
Went down behind the western hill to die.

Now Wolfram, when the rumour reach'd his ears
That, from their quest of saving grace return'd,
The pilgrims all within the castle court
Were gather'd, flock'd about by happy friends,
Pass'd from his portal swiftly, and ran out
And join'd the clustering crowd. Full many a face,
Wasted and wan, he recogniz'd, and clasp'd
Full many a lean hand clutching at his own,
Of those who, stretch'd upon the grass, or propp'd
Against the boulder-stones, were press'd about
By weeping women, clamorous to unbind
Their sandal-thongs and bathe the bruisèd feet.

Then up and down, and swiftly through and through,
And round about, skirting the crowd, he hurried,
With greetings fair to all; till, fill'd with fear,
Half-hopeless of his quest, yet harbouring hope,
He paused perplex'd beside the castle gates.
There, at his side, the youngest of the train,
A blue-eyed pilgrim tarried, and to him
Turn'd Wolfram questioning of Tannhäuser's fate;
And learnt in few words how, his sin pronounced
Deadly and irremediable, the knight
Had faded from before the awful face
Of Christ's incensèd Vicar; and none knew
Whither he wander'd, to what desolate lands,
Hiding his anguish from the eyes of men.
Then Wolfram groan'd, and clasp'd his hands, and cried
'Merciful God!' and fell upon his knees
In purpose as of prayer—but, suddenly,
About the gate the crowd moved, and a cry

Went up for space, when, rising, he beheld

Four maids who on a pallet bore the form

Of wan Elizabeth. The whisper grew

That she had met the pilgrims, and had learn'd

Tannhäuser's fate, and fall'n beside the way.

And Wolfram, in the ghastly torchlight, saw

The white face of the Princess turn'd to his,

And for a space their eyes met; then she raised

One hand towards Heaven, and smiled as who should say,

' O friend, I journey unto God; farewell!'

But he could answer nothing; for his eyes

Were blinded by his tears, and through his tears

Dimly, as in a dream, he saw her borne

Up the broad granite steps that wind within

The palace; and his inner eye, entranced,

Saw in a vision four great Angels stand,

Expectant of her spirit, at the foot

Of flights of blinding brilliancy of stairs

Innumerable, that through the riven skies
Scaled to the City of the Saints of God.
Then, when thick night fell on his soul, and all
The vision fled, he solitary stood
A crazèd man within the castle-court;
Whence issuing, with wild eyes and wandering gait,
He through the darkness, groaning, pass'd away.

All that lone night, along the haunted hills,
By dizzy brinks of mountain precipices,
He fleeted, aimless as an unused wind
That wastes itself about a wilderness.
Sometimes from low-brow'd caves, and hollow crofts
Under the hanging woods, there came and went
A voice of wail upon the midnight air,
As of a lost soul mourning; and the voice
Was still the voice of his remember'd friend.
Sometimes (so fancy mock'd the fears she bred!)

He heard along the lone and eery land
Low demon laughters; and a sullen strain
Of horror swell'd upon the breeze; and sounds
Of wizard dance, with shawm and timbrel, flew
Ever betwixt waste air and wandering cloud
O'er pathless peaks.   Then, in the distance toll'd,
Or seem'd to toll, a knell: the breezes dropp'd:
And, in the sudden pause, that passing bell
With ghostly summons bade him back return
To where, till dawn, a shade among the shades
Of Wartburg, watching one lone tower, he saw
A light that waned with all his earthly hopes.
The calm Dawn came and from the eastern cliff,
Athwart the glistening slopes and cold green copse,
Call'd to him, careless of a grief not hers;
But he, from all her babbling birds, and all
Her vexing sunlight, with a weary heart
Drew close the darkness of the glens and glades

About him, flying through the forest deeps.

And day and night, dim eve and dewy dawn,

Three times returning, went uncared for by ;

And thrice the double twilights rose and fell

About a land where nothing seem'd the same,

At eve or dawn, as in the time gone by.

But, when the fourth day like a stranger slipp'd

To his unhonour'd grave, God's Angel pass'd

Across the threshold of the Landgrave's hall,

And in his bosom bore to endless peace

The weary spirit of Elizabeth.

Then, in that hour when Death with gentle hand

Had droop'd the quiet eyelids o'er the eyes

That Wolfram loved, to Wolfram's heart there came

A calmness like the calmness of a grave

Wall'd safe from all the noisy walks of men

In some green place of peace where daisies grow.

His tears fell in the twilight with the dews,

Soft as the dews that with the twilight fell,
When, over scarr'd and weather-wounded walls,
Sharp-jaggèd mountain cones, and tangled quicks,
Eve's spirit, settling, laid the land to sleep
In skyey trance. Nor yet less soft to fuse
Memory with hope, and earth with heaven, to him,
Athwart the harsher anguish of that day,
There stole with tears the tender human sense
Of heavenly mercy. Through that milder mood,
Like waifs that float to shore when storms are spent,
Flow'd to his heart old memories of his friend,
O'erwoven with the weed of other griefs,
Of other griefs for her that grieved no more—
And of that time when, like a blazing star
That moves and mounts between the Lyre and Crown,
Tannhäuser shone; ere sin came, and with sin
Sorrow. And now if yet Tannhäuser lived
None knew: and if he lived, what hope in life?

And if he lived no more, what rest in death?
But every way the dreadful doom of sin.

Thus, musing much on all the mystery
Of life, and death, and love that will not die,
He wander'd forth, incurious of the way;
Which took the wont of other days, and wound
Along the valley.   Now the nodding star
Of even, and the deep the dewy hour
Held all the sleeping circle of the hills;
Nor any cloud the stainless heavens obscured,
Save where, o'er Hörsel folded in the frown
Of all his wicked woods, a fleecy fringe
Of vapour veil'd the slowly sinking moon.
There, in the shade, the stillness, o'er his harp
Leaning, of love, and life, and death he sang
A song to which from all her aëry caves
The mountain echo murmur'd in her sleep.

But, as the last strain of his solemn song
Died off among the solitary stars,
There came in answer from the folded hills
A note of human woe. He turn'd, he look'd
That way the sound came o'er the lonely air;
And, seeing, yet believed not that he saw,
But, nearer moving, saw indeed hard-by,
Dark in the darkness of a neighbouring hill,
Lying among the splinter'd stones and stubs
Flat in the fern, with limbs diffused as one
That, having fallen, cares to rise no more,
A pilgrim; all his weeds of pilgrimage
Hanging and torn, his sandals stain'd with blood
Of bruisèd feet, and, broken in his hand,
His wreathèd staff.
              And Wolfram wistfully
Look'd in his face, and knew it not. 'Alas!

Not him,' he murmur'd, 'not my friend!' And then,
'What art thou, pilgrim? whence thy way? how fall'n
In this wild glen? at this lone hour abroad
When only Grief is stirring?' Unto whom
That other, where he lay in the long grass,
Not rising, but with petulant gesture, 'Hence!
Whate'er I am, it skills not. Thee I know
Full well, Sir Wolfram of the Willow-brook,
The Well-belovèd Singer!'

        Like a dart
From a friend's hand that voice thro' Wolfram went:
For memory over all the ravaged form
Wherefrom it issued, wandering, fail'd to find
The man she mourn'd; but Wolfram, to the voice
No stranger, started smit with pain, as all
The past on those sharp tones came back to break
His heart with hopeless knowledge. And he cried,
'Alas, my brother!' Such a change, so drear,

In all so unlike all that once he was
Show'd the lost knight Tannhäuser, where he lay
Fallen across the split and morsell'd crags
Like a dismantled ruin.   And Wolfram said,
' O lost! how comest thou, unabsolved, once more
Among these valleys visited by death,
And shadow'd with the shadow of thy sin?'
Whereto in scorn Tannhäuser, ' Be at rest
O fearful in thy righteousness! not thee,
Nor grace of thine, I seek.'
                              Speaking, he rose
The spectre of a beauty waned away;
And, like a hollow echo of himself
Mocking his own last words, he murmur'd, ' Seek!
' Alas! what seek I here, or anywhere?
Whose way of life is like the crumbled stair
That winds and winds about a ruin'd tower,
And leads no-whither!'

But Wolfram cried, 'Yet turn!
'For, as I live, I will not leave thee thus.
My life shall be about thee, and my voice
Lure scared Hope back to find a resting-place
Even in the jaws of Death. I do adjure thee,
By all that friendship yet may claim, declare
That, even though unabsolved, not uncontrite,
Thy soul no more hath lapsed into the snare
Of that disastrous sorcery. Bid me hail,
Seen through the darkness of thy desolation,
Some light of purer purpose; since I deem
Not void of purpose hast thou sought these paths
That range among the places of the past;
And I will make defeat of Grief with such
True fellowship of tears as shall disarm
Her right hand of its scorpions; nor in vain
My prayers with thine shall batter at the gates

Of Mercy, through all antagonisms of fate
Forcing sharp inlet to her throne in Heaven.'

Whereat Tannhäuser, turning tearless eyes
On Wolfram, murmur'd mournfully, ' If tears
' Fiery as those from fallen seraphs distill'd,
Or centuries of prayers for pardon sigh'd
Sad, as of souls in purgatorial glooms,
Might soften condemnation, or restore
To her, whom most on earth I have offended,
The holy freight of all her innocent hopes
Wreck'd in this ruin'd venture, I would weep
Salt oceans from these eyes. But I no more
May drain the deluge from my heart, no more
On any breath of sigh or prayer rebuild
The rainbow of discovenanted Hope.
Thou, therefore, Wolfram—for her face, when mine
Is dark for ever, thine eyes may still behold—

G

Tell her, if thou unblamed may'st speak of one
Sign'd cross by the curse of God and cancell'd out,
How, at the last, though in remorse of all
That makes allegiance void and valueless,
To me has come, with knowledge of my loss,
Fealty to that pure passion, once betray'd,
Wherewith I loved, and love her.'

        There his voice,
Even as a wave that, touching on the shore
To which it travell'd, is shiver'd and diffused,
Sank, scatter'd into spray of wasteful sighs,
And back dissolved into the deeper grief.

To whom, Wolfram, 'Oh answer by the faith
In which mankind are kindred, art thou not
From Rome, unhappiest?' 'From Rome? ah me!'
He mutter'd, 'Rome is far off, very far,

And weary is the way!' But undeterr'd
Wolfram renew'd, 'And hast thou not beheld
The face of Christ's High Vicar?' And again,
'Pass on,' he mutter'd, 'what is that to thee?'
Whereto, with sorrowful voice, Wolfram, 'O all,
And all in all to me that love my friend!'
'My friend!' Tannhäuser laugh'd a bitter laugh.
Then sadlier said, 'What thou would'st know, once known,
'Will cause thee to recall that wasted word
And cancel all the kindness in thy thoughts;
Yet shalt thou learn my misery, and learn
The man so changed, whom once thou calledst "friend,"
That unto him the memory of himself
Is as a stranger.' Then, with eyes that swam
True sorrow, Wolfram stretch'd his arms and sought
To clasp Tannhäuser to him: but the other
Waved him away, and with a shout that sprang
Fierce with self-scorn from misery's deepest depth,

'Avaunt!' he cried, 'the ground whereon I tread,
Is ground accurst!
            'Yet stand not so far off
But what thine ears, if yet they will, may take
The tale thy lips from mine have sought to learn;
Then, sign thyself, and peaceful go thy ways.'
And Wolfram, for the grief that choked his voice,
Could only murmur 'Speak!' But for a while
Tannhäuser to sad silence gave his heart;
Then fetch'd back some far thought, sighing, and said:

'O Wolfram, by the love of lovelier days
Believe I am not so far fallen away
From all I was while we might yet be friends,
But what these words, haply my last, are true:
True as my heart's deep woe what time I felt
Cold on my brow tears wept, and wept in vain,
For me, among the scorn of alter'd friends,

Parting that day for Rome. Remember this:
That when, in the after years to which I pass
A by-word, and a mockery, and no more,
Thou, honour'd still by honourable men,
Shalt hear my name dishonour'd, thou may'st say,
" Greatly he grieved for that great sin he sinn'd."

' Ever, as up the windy alpine way,
We halting oft by cloudy convent doors,
My fellow pilgrims warm'd themselves within,
And ate and drank, and slept their sleep, all night
I, fasting, slept not; but in ice and snow
Wept, aye remembering her that wept for me,
And loath'd the sin within me. When at length
Our way lay under garden terraces
Strewn with their dropping blossoms, thick with scents,
Among the towers and towns of Italy,
Whose sumptuous airs along them, like the ghosts

Of their old gods, went sighing, I nor look'd
Nor linger'd, but with bandaged eyeballs prest,
Impatient, to the city of the shrine
Of my desired salvation. There by night
We enter'd. There, all night, forlorn I lay
Bruised, broken, bleeding, all my garments torn,
And all my spirit stricken with remorse,
Prostrate beneath the great cathedral stairs.
So the dawn found me. From a hundred spires
A hundred silvery chimes rang joy: but I
Lay folded in the shadow of my shame,
Darkening the daylight from me in the dust.
Then came a sound of solemn music flowing
To where I crouch'd; voices and trampling feet:
And, girt by all his crimson cardinals,
In all his pomp the sovran Pontiff stood
Before me in the centre of my hopes;
Which trembled round him into glorious shapes,

Golden, as clouds that ring the risen sun.
And all the people, all the pilgrims, fell
Low at his sacred feet, confess'd their sins,
And, pardon'd, rose with psalms of jubilee
And confident glad faces.
      ' Then I sprang
To where he paused above me; with wild hands
Clutch'd at the skirts I could not reach; and sank
Shiveringly back; crying, " O holy, and high,
And terrible, that hast the keys of heaven !
Thou that dost bind and dost unloose, from me,
For Mary's sake, and the sweet Saints, unbind
The grievous burthen of the curse I bear."
And when he question'd, and I told him all
The sin that smoulder'd in my blood, how bred,
And all the strangeness of it, then his face
Was as the Judgment Angel's; and I hid
My own; and, hidden from his eyes, I heard:

' " Hast thou within the nets of Satan lain?
Hast thou thy soul to her perdition pledged?
Hast thou thy lip to Hell's Enchantress lent,
To drain damnation from her reeking cup?
Then know that sooner from the wither'd staff
That in my hand I hold green leaves shall spring,
Than from the brand in hell-fire scorch'd rebloom
The blossoms of salvation."

' The voice ceased,
' And, with it all things from my sense. I waked
I know not when, but all the place was dark:
Above me, and about me, and within
Darkness: and from that hour by moon or sun
Darkness unutterable as of death
Where'er I walk. But death himself is near!
Oh, might I once more see her, unseen; unheard,
Hear her once more; or know that she forgives

Whom Heaven forgives not, nor his own lost peace;
I think that even among the nether fires
And those dark fields of Doom to which I pass,
Some blessing yet would haunt me.'
                                        Sorrowfully
He rose among the tumbled rocks and lean'd
Against the dark. As one that many a year,
Sunder'd by savage seas unsociable
From kin and country, in a desert isle
Dwelling till half dishumaniz'd, beholds
Haply, one eve, a far-off sail go by,
That brings old thoughts of home across his heart;
And still the man who thinks—' They are all gone,
Or changed, that loved me once, and I myself
No more the same'—watches the dwindling speck
With weary eyes, nor shouts, nor waves a hand;
But after, when the night is left alone,
A sadness falls upon him, and he feels

More solitary in his solitudes,
And tears come starting fast; so, tearful, stood
Tannhäuser, whilst his melancholy thoughts,
From following up far-off a waning hope,
Back to himself came, one by one, more sad
Because of sadness troubled.

                        Yet not long
He rested thus; but murmur'd, 'Now, farewell!
'I go to hide me darkly in the groves
That she was wont to haunt; where some sweet chance
Haply may yield me sight of her, and I
May stoop, she pass'd away, to kiss the ground
Made sacred by her passage ere I die.'
But him departing Wolfram held, 'Vain! vain!
'Thy footstep sways with fever, and thy mind
Wavers within thy restless eyes. Lie here,
O unrejected, in my arms, and rest!'

Now o'er the cumbrous hills began to creep
A thin and watery light: a whisper went
Vague through the vast and dusky-volum'd woods:
And, uncompanion'd, from a drowsy copse
Hard-by a solitary chirp came cold:
While, spent with inmost trouble, Tannhäuser lean'd
His wan cheek pillow'd upon Wolfram's breast,
Calm, as in death, with placid lids down lock'd.
And Wolfram pray'd within his heart, ' Ah, God!
' Let him not die, not yet, not thus, with all
The sin upon his spirit!' But while he pray'd
Tannhäuser raised delirious looks, and sigh'd,
' Hearest thou not the happy songs they sing me?
Seëst thou not the lovely floating forms?
O fair, and fairer far than fancy fashion'd!
O sweet the sweetness of the songs they sing!
For thee, . . . they sing . . . the goddess waits: for thee

With braided blooms the balmy couch is strewn,

And loosed for thee . . . they sing . . . *the golden zone.*

Fragrant for thee the lighted spices fume

With streaming incense sweet, and sweet for thee

The scatter'd rose, the myrtle crown, the cup,

The nectar-cup for thee! . . . they sing. *Return,*

Though late, too long desired, . . . I hear them sing,

Delay no more delights too long delay'd:

Turn to thy rest; . . . they sing . . . *the married doves*

Murmur; the Fays soft-sparkling tapers tend;

The odours burn the purple bowers among;

And Love for thee, and Beauty, waits! . . . they sing.'

'Ah me! ah madman!' Wolfram cried, 'yet cram

Thy cheated ears, nor chase with credulous heart

The fair dissembling of that dream. For thee

Not roses now, but thorns; nor myrtle wreath,

But cypress rather and the graveyard flower

Befitting saddest brows; nor nectar pour'd,
But prayers and tears! For thee in yonder skies
An Angel strives with Sin and Death; for thee
Yet pleads a spirit purer than thine own:
For she is gone! gone to the breast of God!
Thy Guardian Angel, while she walk'd the earth,
Thine intercessionary Saint while now
For thee she sues about the Throne of Thrones,
Beyond the stars, our star, Elizabeth!'

Then Wolfram felt the shatter'd frame that lean'd
Across his breast with sudden spasms convulsed.
'Dead! is she dead?' Tannhäuser murmur'd, 'dead!
Gone to the grave, so young! murder'd—by me!
Dead—and by my great sin! O Wolfram, turn
Thy face from mine. I am a dying man!'
And Wolfram answer'd, 'Dying? ah, not thus!
'Yet make one sign thou dost repent the past,

One word, but one! to say thou hast abhorr'd
That false she devil that, with her damnèd charms,
Hath wrought this ruin; and I, though all the world
Roar out against thee, ay! though fiends of hell
Howl from the deeps, yet I, thy friend, even yet
Will cry them " Peace!" and trust the hope I hold
Against all desperate odds, and deem thee saved.'
Whereto Tannhäuser, speaking faintly, ' Friend,
The fiend that haunts in ruins through my heart
Will wander sometimes. In the nets I trip,
When most I fret the meshes. These spent shafts
Are of a sickly brain that shoots awry,
Aiming at something better. Bear with me.
I die: I pass I know not whither: yet know
That I die penitent. O Wolfram, pray,
Pray for my soul! I cannot pray myself.
I dare not hope: and yet I would not die

Without a hope, if any hope, though faint
And far beyond this darkness, yet may dwell
In the dear death of Him that died for all.'

He whispering thus; far in the Aurorean East
The ruddy sun, uprising, sharply smote
A golden finger on the airy harps
By Morning hung within her leafy bowers;
And all about the budded dells, and woods
With sparkling-tassell'd tops, from birds and brooks
A hundred hallelujahs hail'd the light.
The whitethorn glisten'd from the wakening glen:
O'er golden gravel danced the dawning rills:
All the delighted leaves by copse and glade
Gamboll'd; and breezy bleatings came from flocks
Far off in pleasant pastures fed with dew.

But whilst, unconscious of the silent change

Thus stol'n around him, o'er the dying bard
Hung Wolfram, on the breeze there came a sound
Of mourning moving down the narrow glen;
And, looking up, he suddenly was ware
Of four white maidens, moving in the van
Of four black monks who bore upon her bier
The flower-strewn corpse of young Elizabeth.
And after these, from all the castled hills,
A multitude of lieges and of lords;
A multitude of men at arms, with all
Their morions hung with mourning; and in midst,
His worn cheek channell'd with unwonted tears,
The Landgrave, weeping for Elizabeth.
These, as the sad procession nearer wound,
And nearer, trampling bare the feathery weed
To where Sir Wolfram rested o'er his friend,
Tannhäuser caught upon his dying gaze;
And caught, perchance, upon the inward eye,

Far, far beyond the corpse, the bier, and far
Beyond the widening circle of the sun,
Some sequel of that vision Wolfram saw:
The crownèd Spirit by the Jasper Gates;
The four white Angels o'er the walls of Heaven;
The shores where, tideless, sleep the seas of Time
Soft by the City of the Saints of God.

Forth, with the strength that lastly comes to break
All bonds, from Wolfram's folding arm he leapt,
Clamber'd the pebbly path, and, groaning, fell
Flat on the bier of love—his bourn at last!
Then, even then, while question question chased
About the ruffled circle of that grief,
And all was hubbub by the bier, a noise
Of shouts and hymns brake in across the hills,
That now o'erflow'd with hurrying feet; and came,
Dash'd to the hip with travel, and dew'd with haste,

H

A flying post, and in his hand he bore
A wither'd staff o'erflourish'd with green leaves;
Who,—follow'd by a crowd of youth and eld,
That sang to stun with sound the lark in heaven,
' A miracle! a miracle from Rome!
Glory to God that makes the bare bough green!'—
Sprang in the midst, and, hot for answer, ask'd
News of the Knight Tannhäuser.

      Then a monk
Of those that, stoled in sable, bore the bier
Pointing, with sorrowful hand, ' Behold the man!'
But straight the other, ' Glory be to God!
This from the Vicar of the fold of Christ:
The wither'd staff hath flourish'd into leaves,
The brand shall bloom, though burn'd with fire, and tho
—Thy soul from sin be saved!' To whom, with tears
That flash'd from lowering lids, Wolfram replied:
' To him a swifter message, from a source

Mightier than whence thou comest, hath been vouch-
    safed.
See these stark hands, blind eyes, and bloodless lips,
This shatter'd remnant of a once fair form,
Late home of desolation, now the husk
And ruin'd chrysalis of a regal spirit
That up to heaven hath parted on the wing!
But thou, to Rome returning with hot speed,
Tell the high Vicar of the Fold of Christ
How that lost sheep his rescuing hand would reach,
Although by thee unfound, is found indeed,
And in the Shepherd's bosom lies at peace.'

And they that heard him lifted up the voice
And wept. But they that stood about the hills
Far off, not knowing, ceased not to cry out,
' Glory to God that makes the bare bough green!'
Till Echo, from the inmost heart of all

That mellowing morn blown open like a rose
To round and ripen to the perfect noon,
Resounded, 'Glory! glory!' and the rocks
From glen to glen rang, 'Glory unto God!'

And so those twain, sever'd by Life and Sin,
By Love and Death united, in one grave
Slept. But Sir Wolfram pass'd into the wilds:
There, with long labour of his hands, he hew'd
A hermitage from out the hollow rock,
Wherein he dwelt, a solitary man.
There, many a year, at nightfall or at dawn,
The pilgrim paused, nor ever paused in vain,
For words of cheer along his weary way.
But once, upon a windy night, men heard
A noise of rustling wings, and at the dawn
They found the hermit parted to his peace.
The place is yet. The youngest pilgrim knows,

And loves it. Three grey rocks; and, over these,
A mountain ash that, mourning, bead by bead,
Drops her red rosary on a ruin'd cell.

So sang the Saxon Bard. And when he ceased,
The women's cheeks were wet with tears; but all
The broad-blown Barons roar'd applause, and flow'd
The jostling tankards prodigal of wine.

THE END.

LONDON:
PRINTED BY WILLIAM CLOWES AND SONS, STAMFORD STREET
AND CHARING CROSS.

www.ingramcontent.com/pod-product-compliance
Lightning Source LLC
Chambersburg PA
CBHW030404170426
43202CB00010B/1481